VIETNAMESE
FOLK
POETRY

TRANSLATED BY JOHN BALABAN

UNICORN PRESS   GREENSBORO

LC 74-82762   Feb 14 77
ISBN paper 0-87775-066-1
ISBN cloth 0-87775-063-7

Coins of Van-Lich, Harmony in the Kingdom, Autumn, The Body Is Pain, Mo Village Girl, and *Tao* were translated in collaboration with Crystal Eastin, and are printed with permisson. The translator is indebted to Le Van Phuc, to Nguyen Thi Cam, and to Nguyen Thi Phuoc Hao for their help in gathering and understanding these poems. Portions of this book have been previously printed in *After Our War* by John Balaban (Pittsburgh University Press, 1974), *The Nation, The American Poetry Review, Modern Poetry in Translation,* and *Trans Pacific.* The Unicorn Keepsake Series is edited by Teo Savory and designed by Alan Brilliant.

Unicorn Keepsake Series

TABLE OF CONTENTS

INTRODUCTION

Traditional Vietnamese oral poems are generally known as *ca dao* (pronounced 'ka yow' or 'ka zow'), which popularly translates as 'free songs,' free in the sense that the singer can add verse lines without limit as long as he properly links rhymes, word pitches, and meter. In structure these poems are actually highly controlled, with rules for the number of syllables in a line, for the placement of rhymes within the line, and for the regulation of voice pitch which is an inseparable part of the poem to the Vietnamese listener. Presenting these poems in English with approximations of the original rhyme and meter but without means for presenting the tonal pitches or melodies is — to use a metaphor of the North Vietnamese scholar, Nguyen Khac Vien — like 'drawing a bucket of water from a well where the moon is mirrored and unavoidably losing the silvery shine of her light.'

The tradition of *ca dao* is at least a thousand years old; only recently have the poems been written down or recorded. Over the centuries the Vietnamese have entertained, comforted, and instructed themselves by listening to these poems, by polishing and perfecting them, and by passing them on by word of mouth. As a poem is passed down, it acquires a jewel-like quality. The older poems seem perfect and profound; the newer ones are often rough in sentiment and in style. It is a civilized and civilizing poetry. As Confucius noted of the ancient Chinese folk songs recorded in the *Shih Ching*, *ca dao* serve to 'stimulate the mind, train the observation, encourage social intercourse, and enable one to give vent to his complaint.' More than any other body of expression, *ca dao* is reflective of Vietnamese humanism. It is the poetry of the rural villager who is the backbone of Vietnamese society. This unwritten tradition unlike many other Vietnamese literary styles is largely free of Chinese influence. *Ca* *dao* (which are untitled*) include children's game songs, love songs, lullabies, riddles, trade songs, and reveries about philosophical and social orders. In these poems we can best hear what Vietnamese think and feel. With six exceptions all the poems in this Keepsake edition were recorded in the South of Vietnam in 1971 and 1972.

JOHN BALABAN

---

*To avoid cumbersome footnotes, the translator has himself supplied titles for the poems.

LINKED VERSES

The wind plays with the moon; the moon, with the wind.
The moon sets. Who can the wind play with?

The wind plays, plays with the Moonflower.
The bud is yours, but the blossom is mine.

The wind plays with watercress and chives.
A pity that you have a mother, but no father.

The wind plays. How can one please a friend's heart?
The Milky Way is shallow in some places; some places, deep.

THE COLONIAL TROOPS TRANSPORT

The troop ship whistles once; I still waver.
Whistles twice, and I step down into the boat.
Three times, and the transport pushes north.
I grip the iron rail as tears stream forth,
and ask the helmsman for a rag for my tears.
Now the husband is North; the wife, South.

THE SAIGON RIVER

The Saigon River slides past the Old Market,
its broad waters thick with silt. There,
the rice shoots gather a fragrance,
the fragrance of my country home,
recalling my mother home, arousing deep love.

THE POLE AT THE VILLAGE PAGODA

A lantern sways from the Banner Pole,
the East wind rattles its panes.
My love for you is deep-aching, endless.
In the tipped dish, I grind ink for a poem:
a poem...three or four, saying
Wait for. Hope for. Remember. Love.

COINS OF VAN-LICH

Four words have the coins of Van-Lich.
I regret loving you.
You're another's wife, no longer mine.
One hundred areca nuts; a thousand gold sheets:
half to burn for you, my sweet,
the other five hundred will release the oath,
the vows you so easily spoke.
The lock's broken but who had the key?
You no longer listen to me.
We bump shoulders, your hat is silent every time.

The coins of Van-Lich were minted during the reign of Than-Tong (1573-1620).

LEAVING THE VILLAGE

Even when cross planks are nailed down,
bamboo bridges are shakily unsound. Hard going.
Hard going, so push back: to tidal flats to catch crab,
to the river for fish, to our sandy patch for melons.

HARMONY IN THE KINGDOM

When the rice fields lie fallow,
I play the flute lying on the back of my buffalo.
Happy the people with a Thuan-Nghieu king:
Over the land the intelligent mind spreads like the wind.
The Lo waterfalls are transparent, free and high.
We shake off the jacket of the dust of life.

COMPLAINING ABOUT THE SECOND WIFE

A breeze stirs banana leaves behind the house.
You're crazy about your second wife, who neglects the children.
The children; well, with one on each arm,
with which hand shall I draw water, which hand rinse rice?

AUTUMN

Autumn rains blow.
Autumn rains flow.
Leaves slowly fall.
Dead reeds waver.
Blue water. Surface: Smooth paper.
Near waterfalls, schools of fish leap.
Stand where the bank is steep.

LOVE LAMENT

Stepping into the field, sadness fills my deep heart.
Bundling rice sheaves, tears dart in two streaks.
Who made me miss the ferry's leaving?
Who made this shallow creek that parts both sides?

THE BODY IS PAIN

At the outpost three years,
days I guard; my nights the mandarin plans.
Slash bamboo, cut wood stands.
The body is pain. I can't complain.
My food is bamboo, *truc* shoots and plum.
My fuel and only friends are *giang* and *nua* bamboo.
In the well one fish swims lone and free.

THE RED CLOTH

Sad, idle, I think of my dead mother,
her mouth chewing white rice, tongue removing fish bones.
The Red Cloth drapes the mirror frame:
men of one country must show love for each other.

LULLABY

Little one, go to sleep. Sleep soundly.
Mother's gone to market; father ploughs the far field.
Our parents toil for our meals,
rice and clothing, making the land yield a good home.
Grow up, study hard, little one;
tend to our native place, mountains and rivers.
Become worthy of the Lac-Hong race.
Hopes met, our parents' faces will widen in smiles.

TALKING ABOUT BIRDS

Listen. Listen here, all about birds and beasts:
Sexy and alluring? That's the little Moor Hen.
Manner offends? That's nasty Cormorant.
Slaves like an ant, that's the traveling Teal.
Straining to overhear? Drongoes snoop in trees.
Shaky in its knees, the skinny, brown Egret.
Stays at home each night, that's cowardly Snipe.
Hungry for their tripe, the Pelicans carouse.
Hungry by the house; there, the darting Larks.
Pole the shallow bark; Peacock plies his art.
Red crest, blue feathers, that's a jungle Pheasant.
Bickering unpleasant? That's the sneaky Plover.
Got a magic Book of Colors: the Soothsayer Hawk.
Never married, never caught, that's Wanderer Grebe.
Mate long since dead: the poor Widow-Wed.
Heart as thick as lead, that's the teasing Jay.
Eggs, but won't lay? Duckbirds live that way.

Sitting around, talking about kinds of birds,
Offspring grow up and look for each other.
See, the Weaver is clever and wise.
The Owl nests only at the edge of the island.
Watch: the Magpies have brought some news;
If they hover then call, our sisters are coming.
The Crows, now, are really just like us, cawing
From far off, 'Wash up. The journey's over.'

SHIP OF REDEMPTION

The bell of Linh Mu Pagoda tolls,
awakening the drowsy soul,
probing, reminding one of debt,
washing one clean of worldly dust.
A boat crosses to the Western Lands.

VENTURING OUT

Each evening, ducks paddle, egrets fly;
Mister Elephant snaps sugarcane then strides into the jungle.
I'll follow there to strip rattan plaits,
fetching them home to make a sling for you to go peddling.
Selling at no loss: why, that's profit.
Go on, have a look at the sun's face, at the moon's.

A TINY BIRD

A tiny bird with red feathers,
a tiny bird with black beak
drinks up the lotus pond day by day.
Perhaps I must leave you.

MOTHER EGRET

Egrets bear egret sons.
Mother's after shrimp; little one's at home.
Far off has Mother Egret flown
to alight. . .and be roped by Brother Eel!
Nearby's a man in a bamboo keel
sliding through cattails to catch eel and fowl.
Poling clumsily, he rams the prow.
Brother Eel dives; Mother flies off.

EGRET'S DEATH AND FUNERAL PREPARATIONS

Egret died the other night.
There's two grains of rice with three coins;
One coin for the flute and drum.
One for fat to burn in homage.
One for leaves of Lady's Thumb;
bring back, slice fine, honor Egret.

MO VILLAGE GIRL

I am a Mo Village girl.
I wander, sell beer, happen to meet you.
Good jars don't mean good brew.
Clothes well-mended are better than ill-sewn.
Bad beer soon sends you home.
A torn shirt when mended will become new.

TAO

Sad, I blame Mister Sky.
When sad, I laugh. Happy, I cry.
Not a man, in my next life
I'll become a rustling pine
on a cliff in the sky.
Fly with the pines, cool and lonely.

ACROSS THE FIELD OF THE OLD CORPORAL

That girl wears her hair in a chicken's tail.
Grab her tail and ask where her house is.
Her house is under a mulberry tree
over some green beans, looking out from the bridge,
looking across the field of the Old Corporal.
There'll be dried fish, pumpkin, tasty chicken.

DIFFICULTIES AT LOVE

The French ships run in the new canal.
If you love me, don't hesitate now.
If you love me, don't suspect my faith.
The wild goose flies high, difficult to shoot.
The fish in Quynh Pond, hard to catch.

PHOENIXES AND SPARROWS

Phoenixes compete, so do sparrows.
They call before the shrine, behind the pagoda.
I can use men who are loyal, if not elegant.

LOOKING OUT IN ALL DIRECTIONS

Looking up at the sky,
I see thick rainclouds.
Looking down into hell,
I see crowds of faces.
Looking up to Phnom Penh,
I see traced four gold words.
Looking down to Ca Mau,
I see breakers thrash and churn.
How long have you loved me?
Do you know that I love you?

WHISKY LOVERS

Soft winds circle the mountain head.
Whisky lovers also were bred of the Jade Lord.
From his throne of gold, the Jade Lord
watches them. On his cheeks great tears fork and fall.
Their drinking is convivial.
Unaware, a tippler waltzes off into a pond.

REPLIES

He: In the long river, the fish swim off without a trace.
     If truly wed, a man and woman can wait a thousand years.

She: Who tends the paddy, repairs its dike.
     Whoever has true love will meet. But take care of time.

TESTING THE CONFUCIAN IDEAL

She: King. Father. Mother. Husband. Wife.
      Sat down in one boat; met a storm and sank.
      Dearest, I want to know whom you would save?

He: Standing before Heaven, I cannot lie.
      I would carry my King on my head,
      father and mother on my shoulders.
      And say to you, dear wife, 'Swim here;
      I will carry you on my back
      and with my hands save the boat.'

THE CARP

The stream rills softly, the carp
fans its red tail like the phoenix.
Of all the people in this field,
my heart swells only for you.

THE PAINTING

The stream runs clear to its stones;
the fish swim in sharp outline.
Girl, turn your face for me to draw.
Tomorrow, if we should drift apart,
I shall find you by this picture.

THE MANDARIN WHO COULDN'T DO ANYTHING

Each evening Master Lu sets his fish traps.
Fish and shrimp leap free.
He laughs, flashing his teeth.
At evening, Master Lu ploughs the field.
The buffalo bolts and breaks the yoke.
Lu sits down and folds his arms.

A WOMAN'S HEART

Trang Tu's legendary wife is very much the modern woman.
Her husband wasn't yet buried when she broke the coffin seal,
scooping up a handful of brains to feed her new lover's strange
Oh, a deep sea and a deep river are easy to plumb.
A woman's heart, although shallow, is hard to probe.

HUSBAND AND WIFE

The oriole eats yellow berries.
The fighting fish knows its bowl.
Husband and wife know their bodies' smell.

IMPOSSIBLE TASKS

Look at the sky: two doves are chasing.
Look into the sea: two fish are racing about.
Go back and build an altar for the King.
Construct a smaller one to honor mother.
Then for my father build a large pagoda.
Go back and sell the banyan's holy soil.
Sell off two old buffaloes. Then I'll marry you.

WICKED WOMEN

Girl, stop pretending tragedy,
curling the tip of your tongue to charm me.
You're no different from the sly Dac Ky
weeping beside her deceived King Tru.
The histories are full of that stuff.
A wild pig can be precious.
Wicked women have fickle minds.
The hen needs a cock and abandons her chicks.
The aroused dove neglects her old nest.
In the water-palm the moor hen pecks open her eggs.
It's all no different from the female crab
who pinches her male when he's lost his shell.

AT THE EXILED KING'S RIVER PAVILION

Evening, before the King's pavilion:
people are sitting, fishing, sad and grieving,
loving, in love, remembering, waiting, watching.
Whose boat plies the river mists?
—offering so many rowing songs
that move these mountains and rivers, our Nation.

BIOGRAPHICAL NOTE ABOUT THE TRANSLATOR

John Balaban was born in 1943 in Philadelphia. He attended the Pennsylvania State University and Harvard and now teaches writing at the former. In 1967 he began a two-year service as a conscientious objector in South Vietnam, first as an instructor at the University of Can Tho, and then as a field representative for the Committee of Responsibility to Save War-Injured Children. His work in Vietnam involved a documentary film ('An Evil Hour,' co-directed with Peter Wolff), Senate testimony before the Subcommittee on Refugees, Civilian Casualties and Escapees, translations and articles. A book of his own poetry, entitled *After Our War*, was published this year by the University of Pittsburgh Press and won the Academy of American Poets' Lamont Award. In 1971 John Balaban returned to South Vietnam and, with the aid of a fellowship from the National Endowment for the Humanities, recorded about five hundred of the traditional *ca dao* poems (an estimated 5000 exist) from about thirty persons, the youngest of whom was a five year old boy, the oldest a seventy-two year old woman. He recorded in the Mekong delta, in Saigon, the Central Highlands, and in Hué. Except for the old imperial city of Hué, the most successful recordings were made in the countryside, away from the erosion of city life. Heavy fighting prevented him from going into many areas. Since his return to North America after nine months of recording in 1971, Balaban has been working on the translations of the poems he recorded, some of which are collected in this volume.

One thousand copies of this edition have been set in Eric Gill's Perpetua type and have been printed on a Vandercook SP-15 Press with Warren's Olde Style paper. Type composition, printing, and binding were done by hand at Unicorn Press, Summer and Autumn, 1974. Members of the Unicorn Work Community during the time that this book was prepared and published were Olivia Allegrone, Karen Benfey, Rachel Benfey, Alan Brilliant, Christie Rucker, Teo Savory, James Weigand, and Elizabeth Wheaton.